POPULAR PIANO SOLOS

Pop Hits, Broadway, Movies and More!

ISBN 978-1-4234-0905-2

WILLIS MUSIC

EXCLUSIVELY DISTRIBUTED BY

7777 W. BLUEMOUND RD. P.O. BOX 13819 MILWAUKEE, WI 53213

Visit Hal Leonard Online at
www.halleonard.com

Contents

Alley Cat

Use with John Thompson's Modern Course for the Piano
SECOND GRADE BOOK, after page 6.

By Frank Bjorn
Arranged by Eric Baumgartner

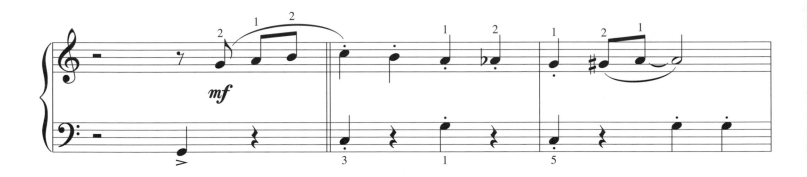

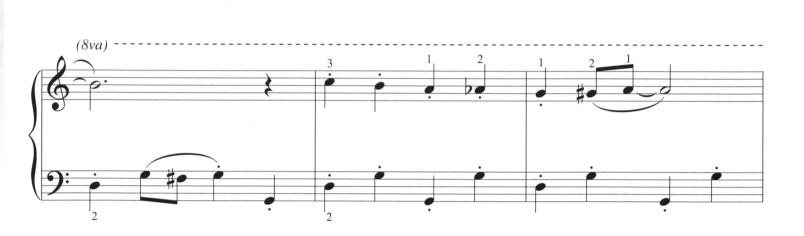

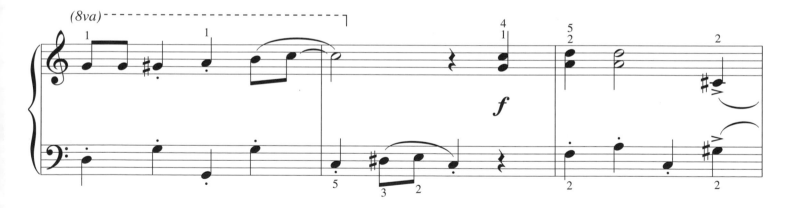

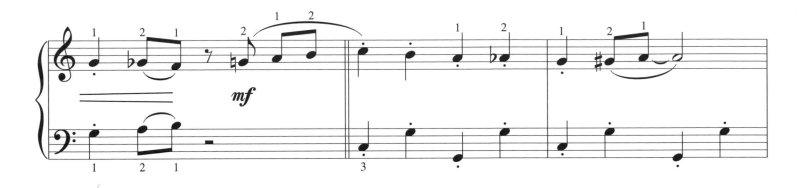

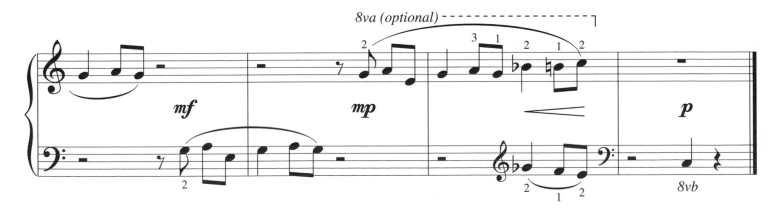

Sway
(Quién Será)

Use after page 11.

English Words by Norman Gimbel
Spanish Words and Music by Pablo Beltrán Ruiz
Arranged by Eric Baumgartner

When ma-rim-ba rhy-thms start to play,

dance with me, — make me sway. — Like the la - zy o - cean

hugs the shore, — hold me close, — sway me more. —

Like a flow-er bend-ing in the breeze, — bend with me, —

sway with ease.＿ When we dance you have a way with me,＿

stay with me,＿ sway with me.＿ Oth - er danc - ers may

be on the floor, dear, but my eyes will see on - ly you.

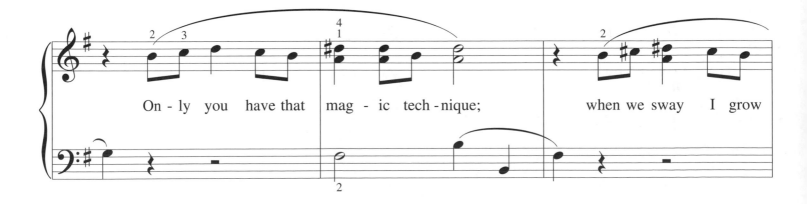

On - ly you have that mag - ic tech - nique; when we sway I grow

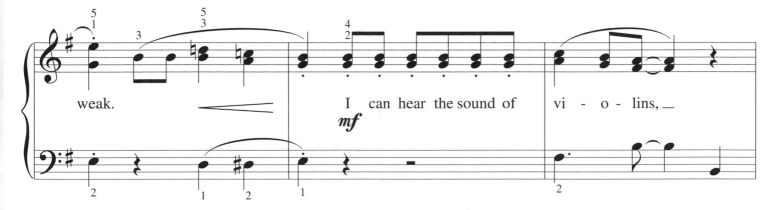

weak.   I can hear the sound of vi - o - lins, __

long be - fore __   it be - gins. __   Make me thrill as on - ly

you know how, __   sway me smooth, __   sway me now. __

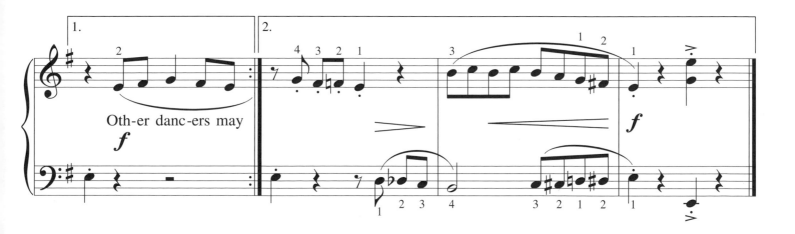

1. Oth-er danc-ers may   2.

My Heart Will Go On

(Love Theme from 'Titanic')

from the Paramount and Twentieth Century Fox Motion Picture TITANIC

Use after page 16.

Music by James Horner
Lyric by Will Jennings
Arranged by Eric Baumgartner

that   is how I   know you   go   on.

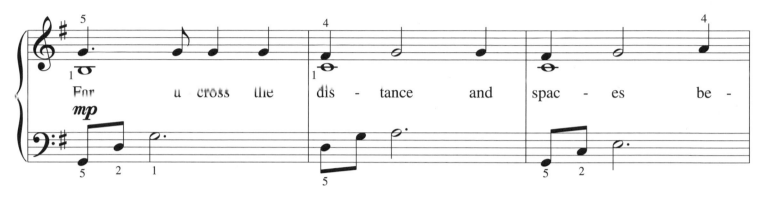

simile

For   a cross the   dis - tance and   spac - es   be -

_mp_

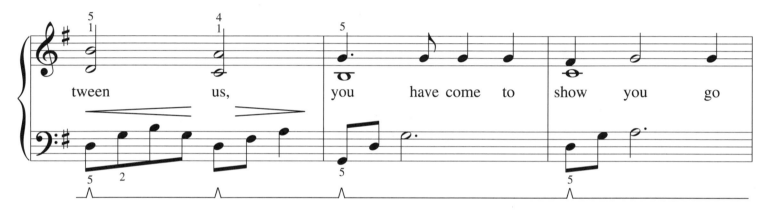

tween   us,   you   have come to   show   you   go

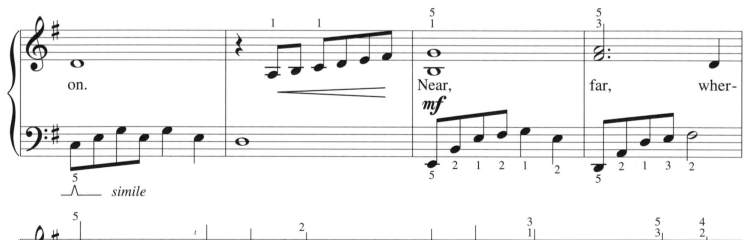

on.   Near,   far,   wher-

simile

_mf_

ev - er you   are,   I   be - lieve   that the

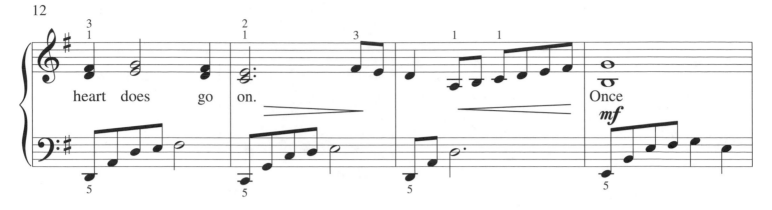

heart does go on. Once

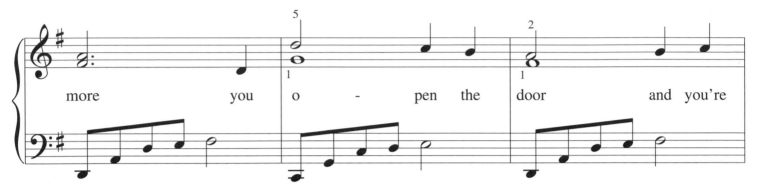

more you o - pen the door and you're

here in my heart, and my heart will go

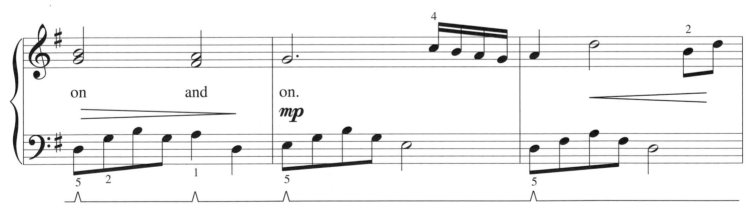

on and on.

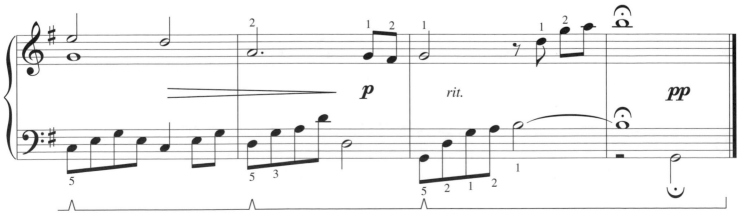

Nadia's Theme

from THE YOUNG AND THE RESTLESS

Use after page 21.

By Barry DeVorzon and Perry Botkin, Jr.
Arranged by Eric Baumgartner

Moderately, with expression

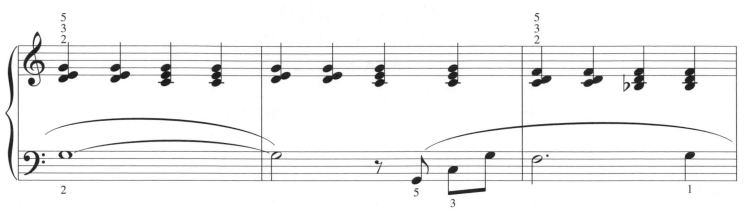

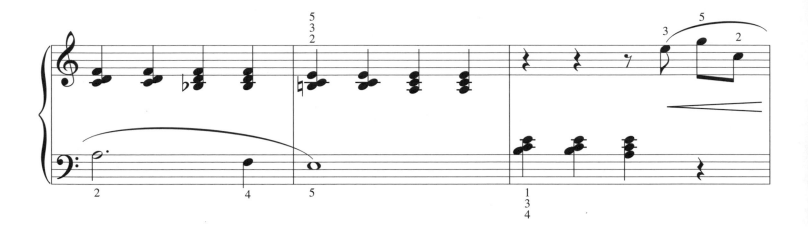

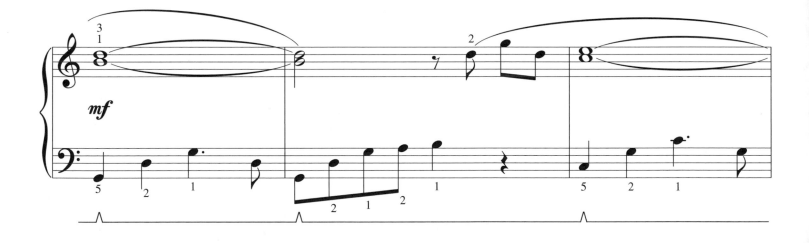

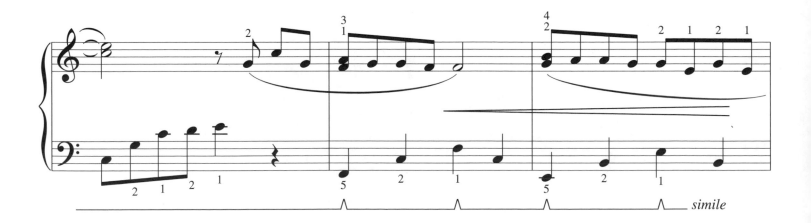

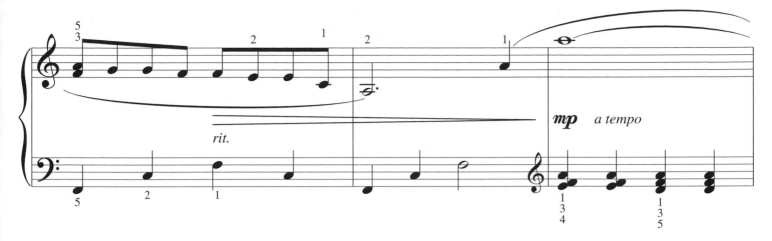

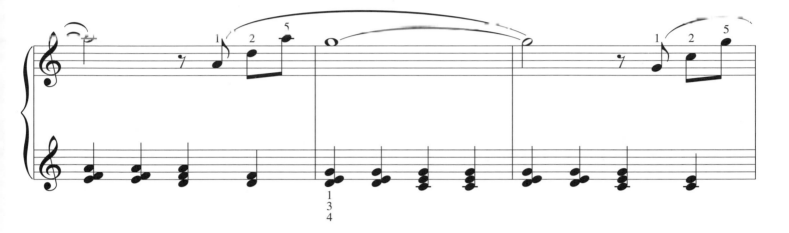

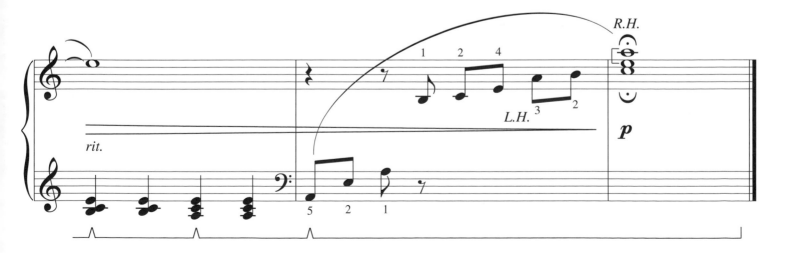

Do-Re-Mi
from THE SOUND OF MUSIC
Use after page 28.

Lyrics by Oscar Hammerstein II
Music by Richard Rodgers
Arranged by Eric Baumgartner

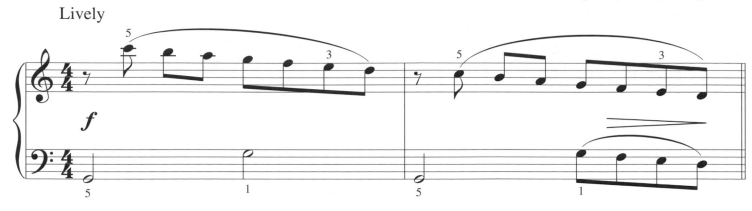

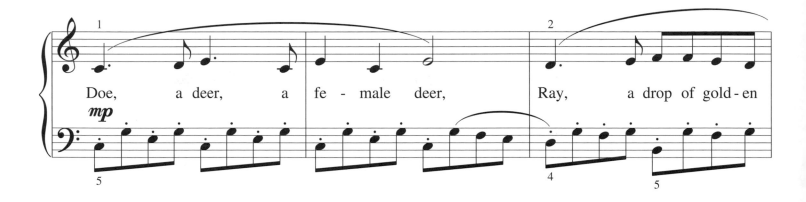

Doe, a deer, a fe-male deer, Ray, a drop of gold-en

sun, Me, a name I call my-self,

Far, a long, long way to run. Sew, a nee-dle pull-ing

thread, La, a note to fol-low sew,

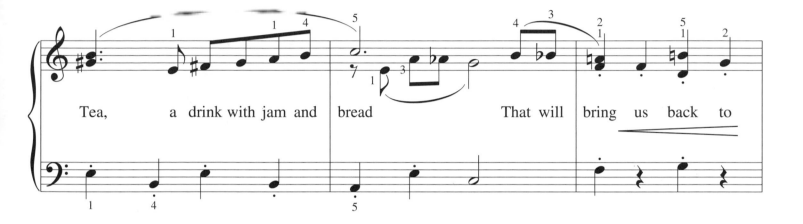

Tea, a drink with jam and bread That will bring us back to

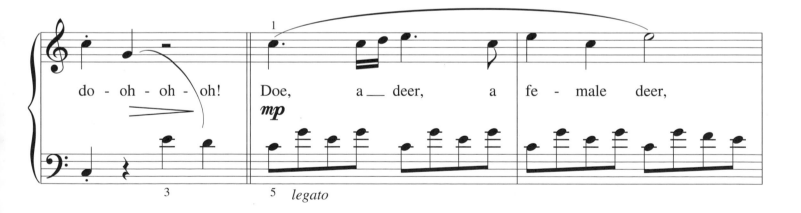

do - oh - oh - oh! Doe, a — deer, a fe - male deer,

mp

legato

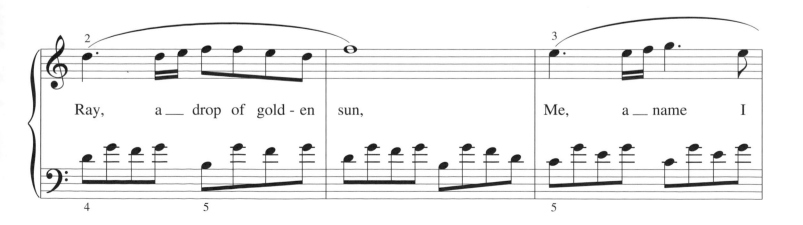

Ray, a — drop of gold - en sun, Me, a — name I

18

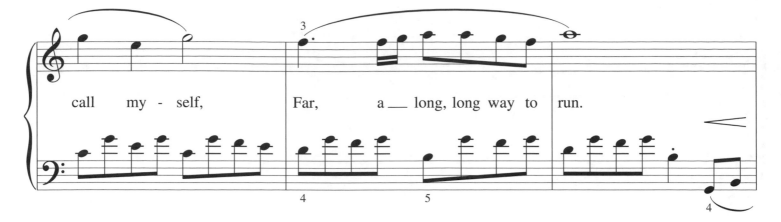

call my - self, Far, a ___ long, long way to run.

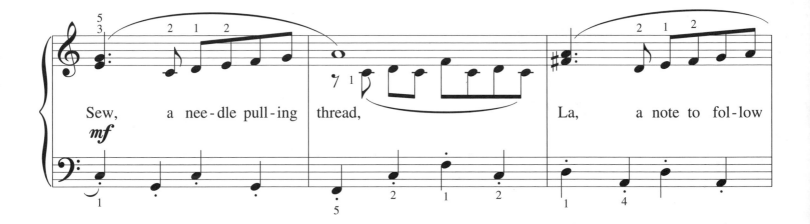

Sew, a nee - dle pull -ing thread, La, a note to fol -low

_mf_

sew, Tea, a drink with jam and bread That will

bring us back to do! Do - re -mi -fa -so -la -ti- do!

_f_

A Time for Us

(Love Theme)

from the Paramount Picture ROMEO AND JULIET

Use after page 35.

Words by Larry Kusik and Eddie Snyder
Music by Nino Rota
Arranged by Eric Baumgartner

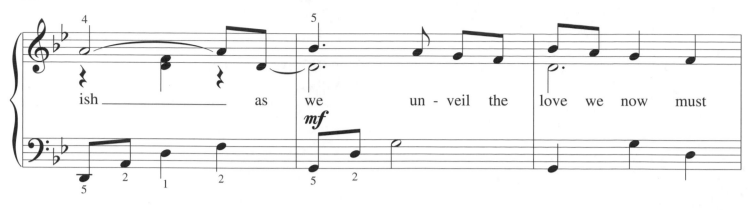

ish _____ as we un - veil the love we now must

hide. _____ A time _____ for us _____ at

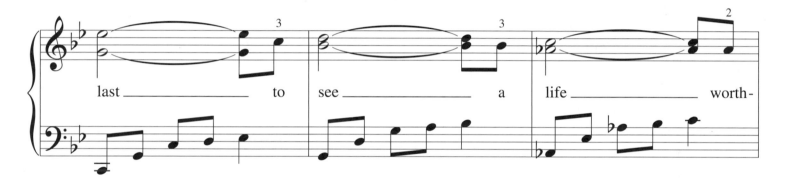

last _____ to see _____ a life _____ worth-

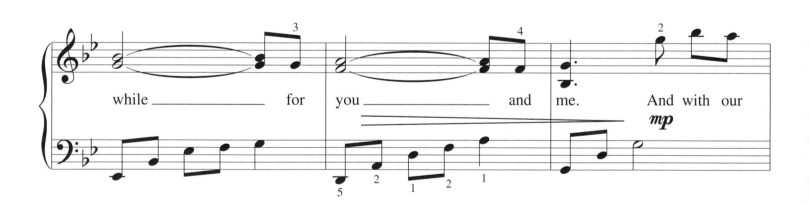

while _____ for you _____ and me. And with our

love through tears and thorns we will en - dure as we pass

sure - ly through ev - 'ry storm. A time for us some - day there'll

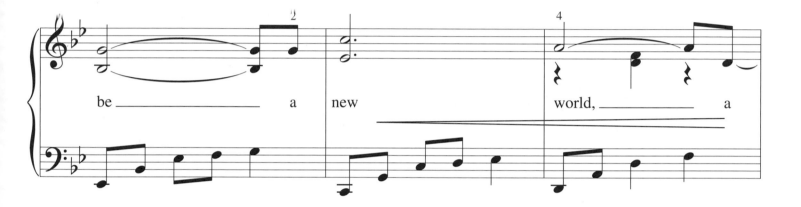

be _____ a new world, _____ a

world of shin - ing hope for you and me.

Raiders March
from the Paramount Motion Picture RAIDERS OF THE LOST ARK
Use after page 45.

Music by John Williams
Arranged by Eric Baumgartner

Triumphantly

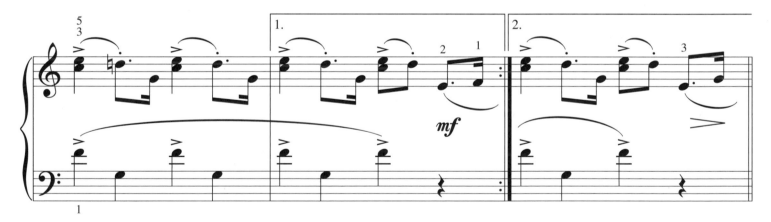

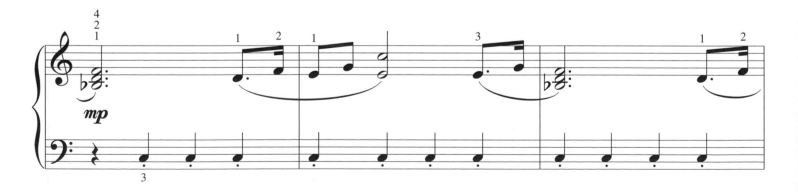

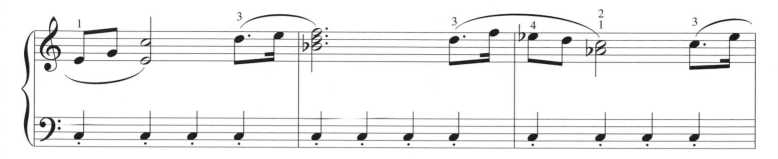

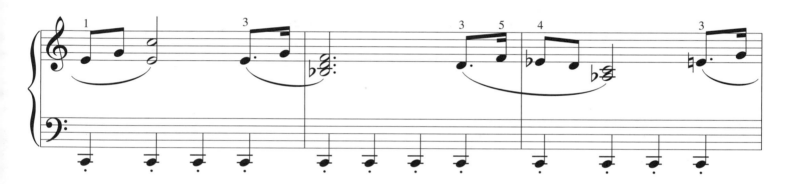

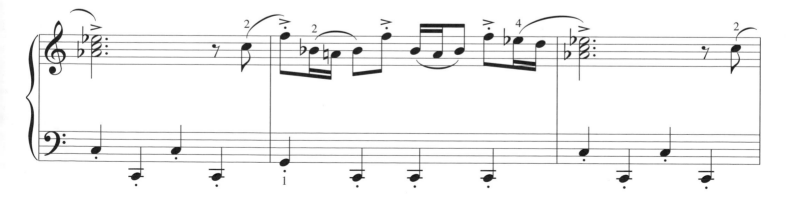

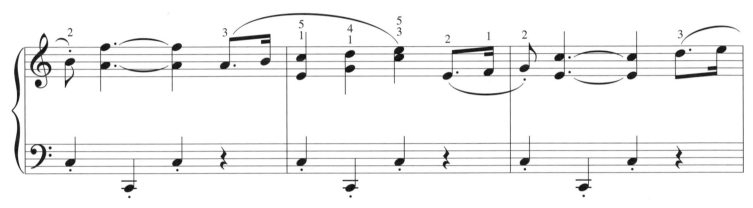

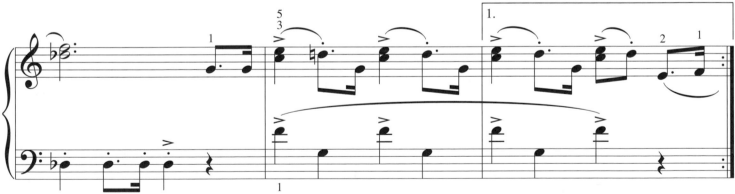

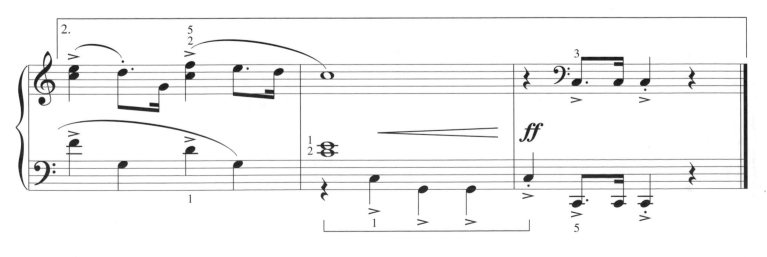

I Could Have Danced All Night

from MY FAIR LADY

Use after page 56.

Words by Alan Jay Lerner
Music by Frederick Loewe
Arranged by Eric Baumgartner

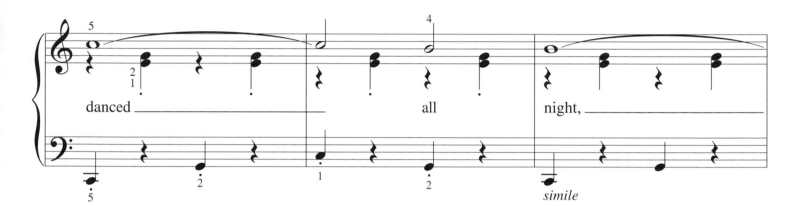

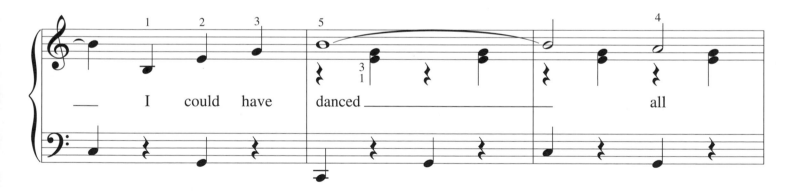

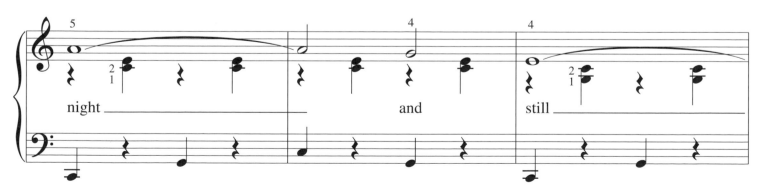

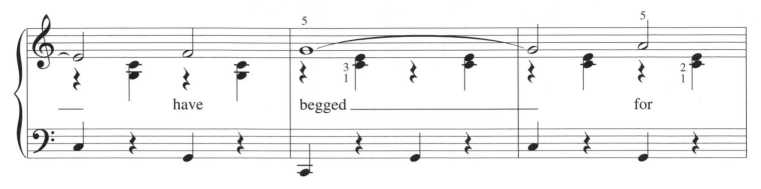

have begged _____ for

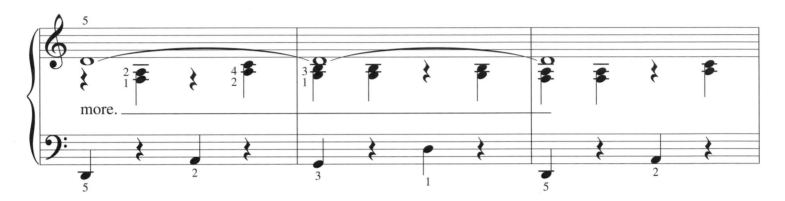

more. _____

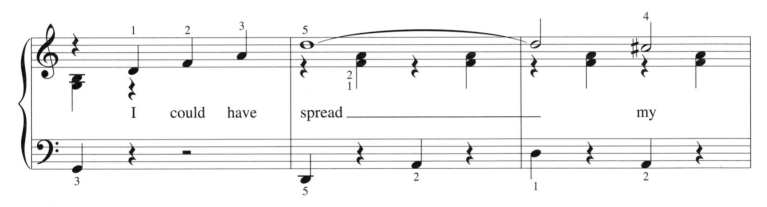

I could have spread _____ my

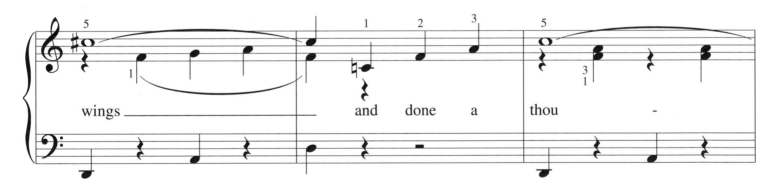

wings _____ and done a thou -

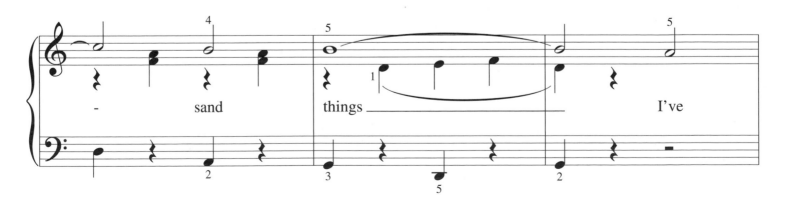

- sand things _____ I've

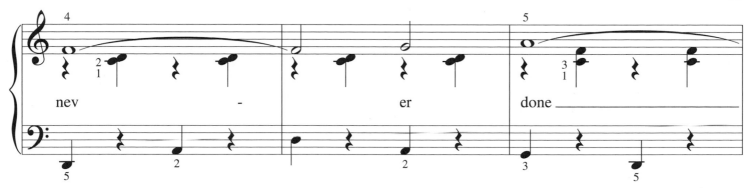

nev - er done _____

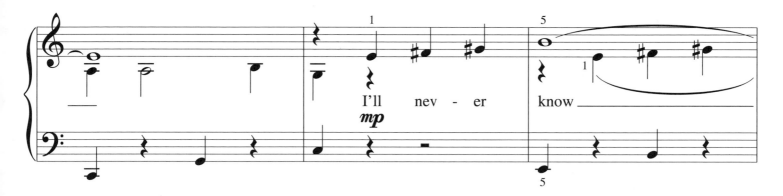

_____ be - fore. _____

_____ I'll nev - er know _____

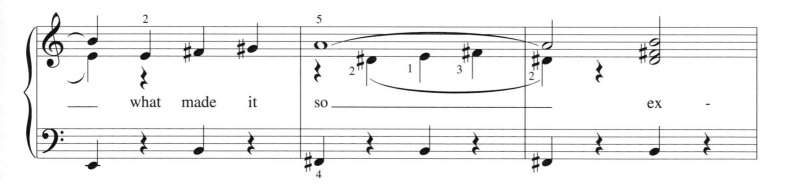

_____ what made it so _____ ex -

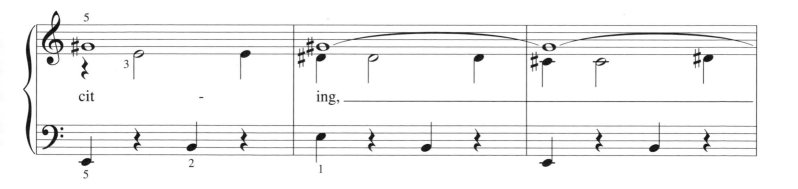

cit - ing, _____

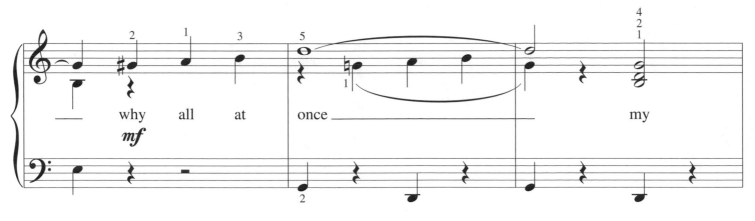

why all at once _____ my

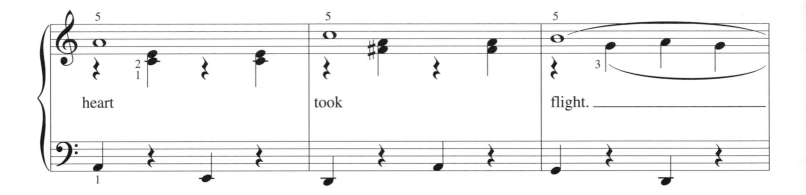

heart took flight. _____

I on - ly

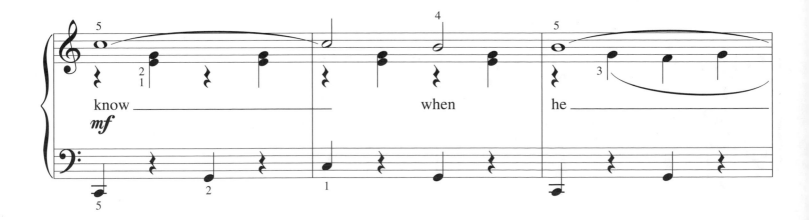

know _____ when he _____

be - gan to dance with

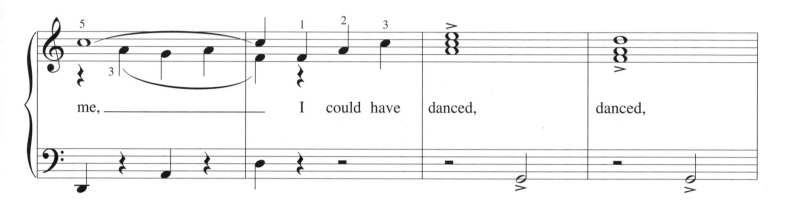

me, I could have danced, danced,

danced all

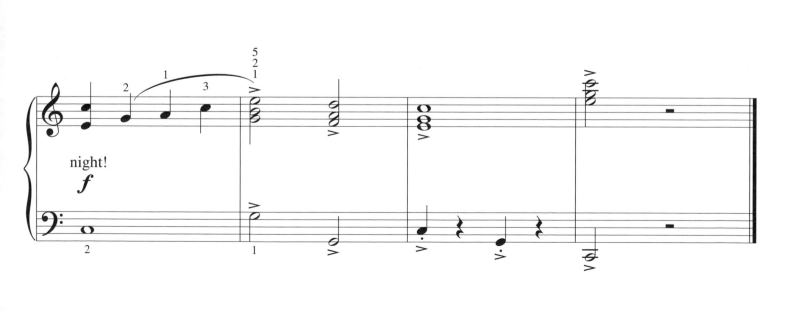

night!

f

Memory
from CATS
Use after page 64.

Music by Andrew Lloyd Webber
Text by Trevor Nunn after T.S. Eliot
Arranged by Eric Baumgartner

with - ered leaves col - lect at my feet

time I knew what hap - pi - ness was, and the

let the

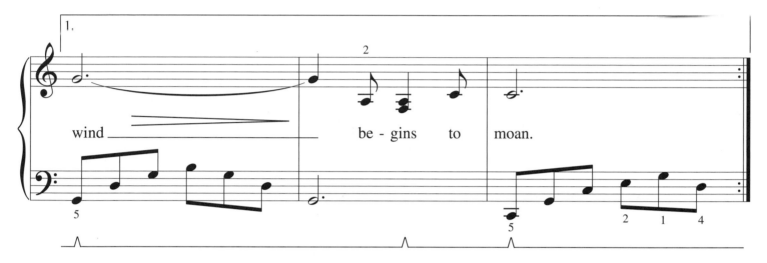

1.

wind be - gins to moan.

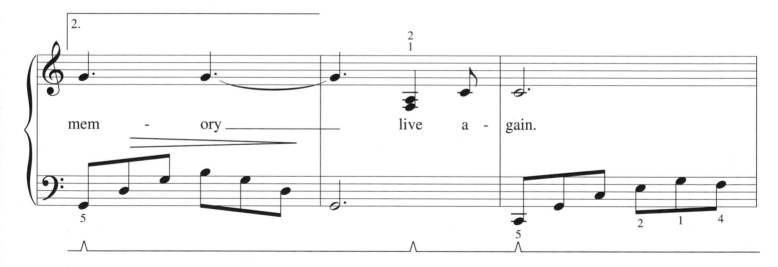

2.

mem - ory live a - gain.

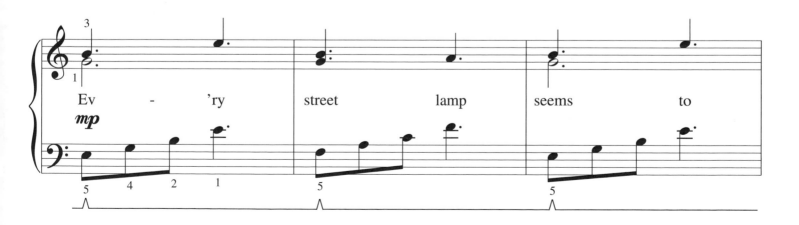

Ev - 'ry street lamp seems to

mp

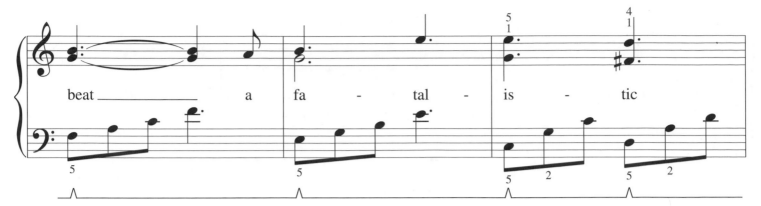

beat _____ a fa - tal - is - tic

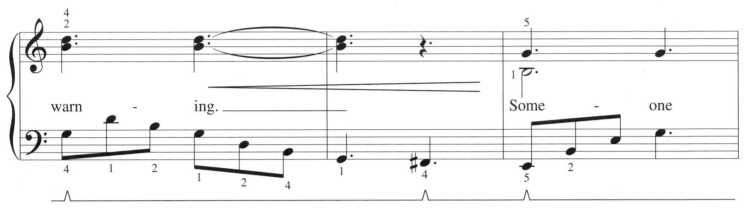

warn - ing. _____ Some - one

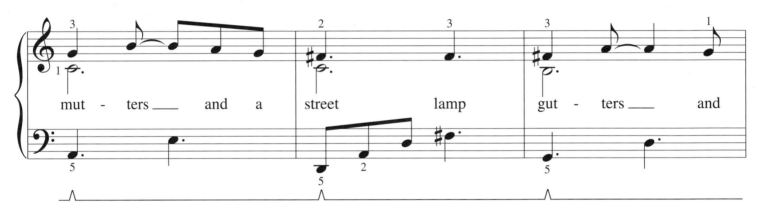

mut - ters ____ and a street lamp gut - ters ____ and

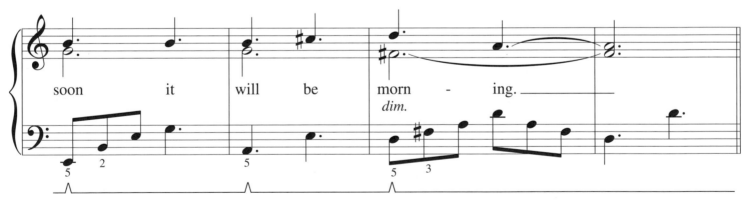

soon it will be morn - ing. _____

dim.

Day - light. _____ I must wait for the sun - rise, _____

mp

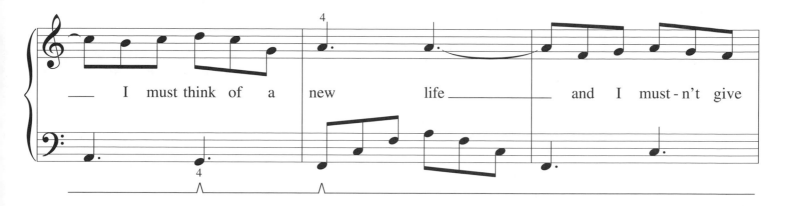

I must think of a new life _____ and I must-n't give

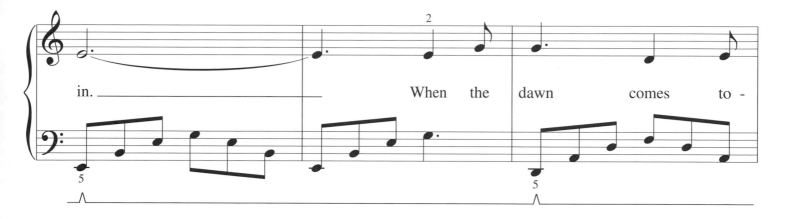

in. _____ When the dawn comes to -

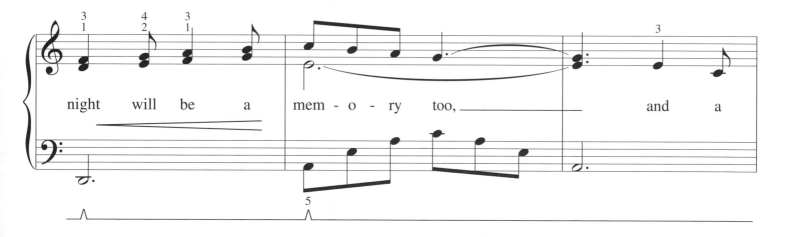

night will be a mem - o - ry too, _____ and a

new day _____ will be - gin.
mp   *molto rit.*   *pp*

The Addams Family Theme

Theme from the TV Show and Movie
Use after page 70.

Music and Lyrics by Vic Mizzy
Arranged by Eric Baumgartner

Playfully

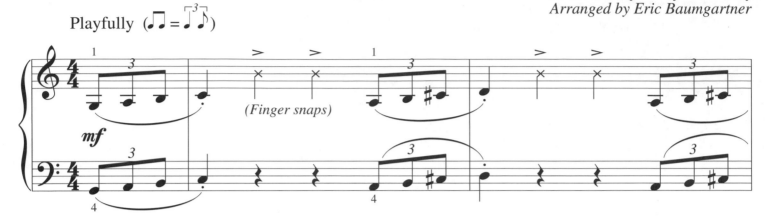

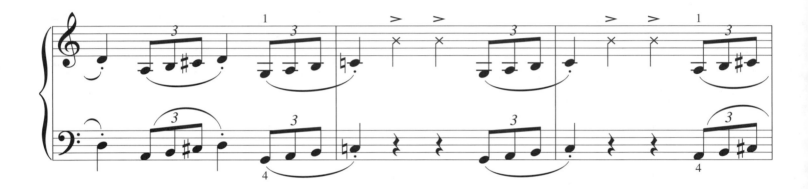

creep-y and they're kook-y, mys - te - ri - ous and spook-y, they're al - to-geth-er ook - y, the

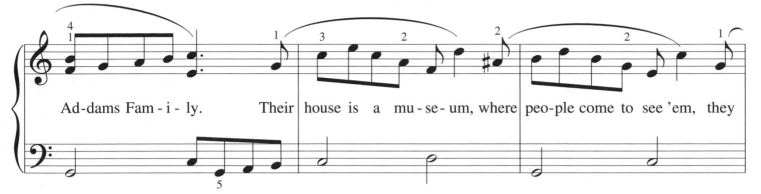

Ad-dams Fam - i - ly.   Their house is a mu-se-um, where peo-ple come to see 'em, they

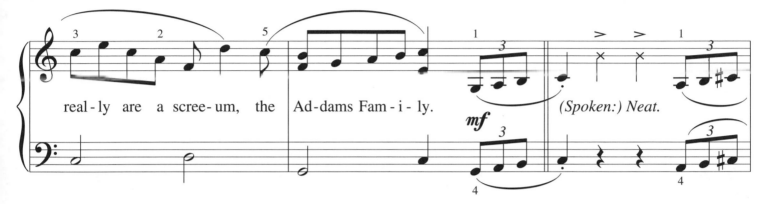

real-ly are a scree-um, the Ad-dams Fam - i - ly.   *mf*   *(Spoken:)* Neat.

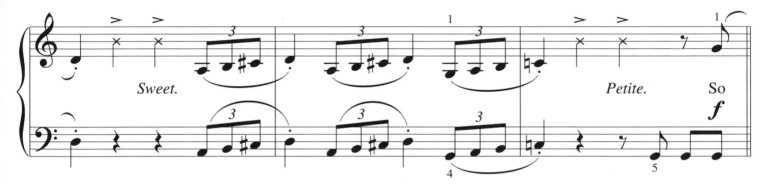

Sweet.   *Petite.*   So

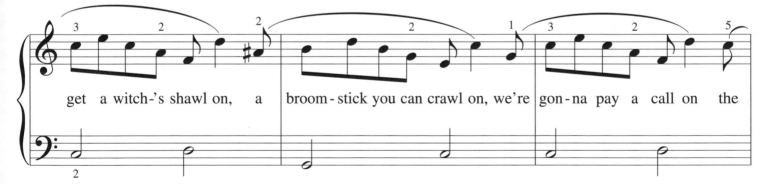

get a witch-'s shawl on, a   broom-stick you can crawl on, we're gon-na pay a call on the

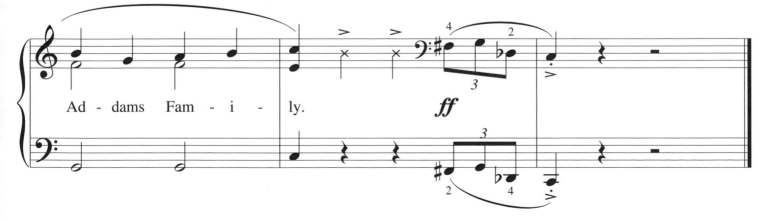

Ad - dams Fam - i - ly.   *ff*

The Masterpiece
the TV Theme from MASTERPIECE THEATRE
Use after page 76.

By J.J. Mouret and Paul Parnes
Arranged by Eric Baumgartner

Majestically

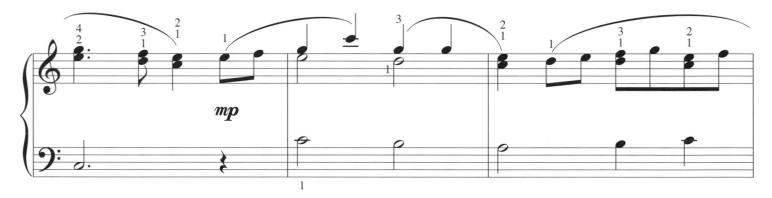

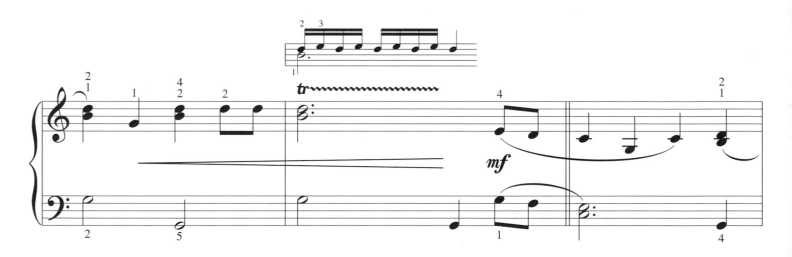

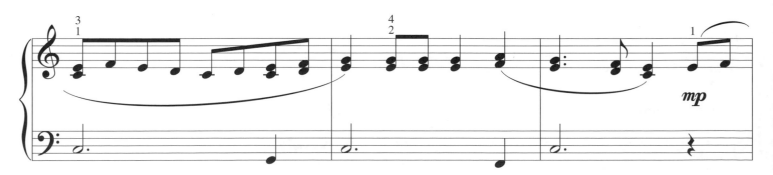

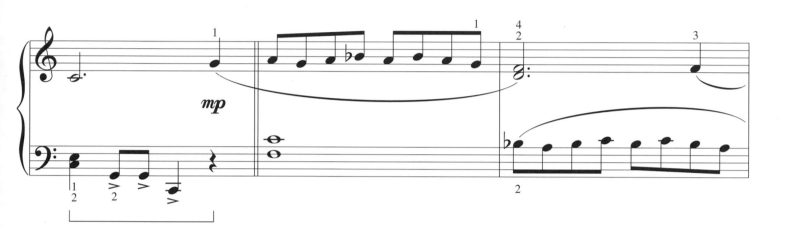

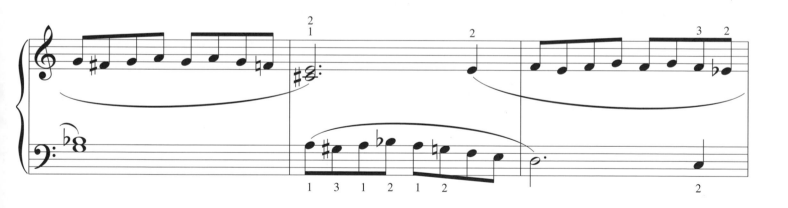

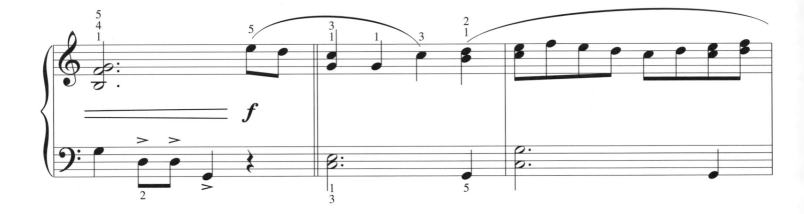

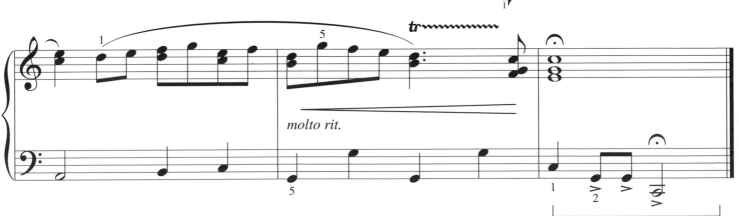

molto rit.

CLASSIC PIANO REPERTOIRE

The *Classic Piano Repertoire* series includes popular as well as lesser-known pieces from a select group of composers out of the Willis piano archives. Every piece has been newly engraved and edited with the aim to preserve each composer's original intent and musical purpose.

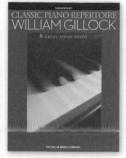

WILLIAM GILLOCK – ELEMENTARY

8 Great Piano Solos

Dance in Ancient Style • Little Flower Girl of Paris • On a Paris Boulevard • Rocking Chair Blues • Sliding in the Snow • Spooky Footsteps • A Stately Sarabande • Stormy Weather.

00416957 ....$8.99

EDNA MAE BURNAM – ELEMENTARY

8 Great Piano Solos

The Clock That Stopped • The Friendly Spider • A Haunted House • New Shoes • The Ride of Paul Revere • The Singing Cello • The Singing Mermaid • Two Birds in a Tree.

00110228 ....$8.99

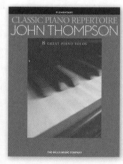

JOHN THOMPSON – ELEMENTARY

9 Great Piano Solos

Captain Kidd • Drowsy Moon • Dutch Dance • Forest Dawn • Humoresque • Southern Shuffle • Tiptoe • Toy Ships • Up in the Air.

00111968 ....$8.99

LYNN FREEMAN OLSON – EARLY TO LATER ELEMENTARY

14 Great Piano Solos

Caravan • Carillon • Come Out! Come Out! (Wherever You Are) • Halloween Dance • Johnny, Get Your Hair Cut! • Jumping the Hurdles • Monkey on a Stick • Peter the Pumpkin Eater • Pony Running Free • Silent Shadows • The Sunshine Song • Tall Pagoda • Tubas and Trumpets • Winter's Chocolatier.

00294722 ....$9.99

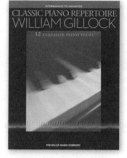

WILLIAM GILLOCK – INTERMEDIATE TO ADVANCED

12 Exquisite Piano Solos

Classic Carnival • Etude in A Major (The Coral Sea) • Etude in E Minor • Etude in G Major (Toboggan Ride) • Festive Piece • A Memory of Vienna • Nocturne • Polynesian Nocturne • Sonatina in Classic Style • Sonatine • Sunset • Valse Etude.

00416912 .... $12.99

EDNA MAE BURNAM – INTERMEDIATE TO ADVANCED

13 Memorable Piano Solos

Butterfly Time • Echoes of Gypsies • Hawaiian Leis • Jubilee! • Longing for Scotland • Lovely Senorita • The Mighty Amazon River • Rumbling Rumba • The Singing Fountain • Song of the Prairie • Storm in the Night • Tempo Tarantelle • The White Cliffs of Dover.

00110229 .... $12.99

JOHN THOMPSON – INTERMEDIATE TO ADVANCED

12 Masterful Piano Solos

Andantino (from Concerto in D Minor) • The Coquette • The Faun • The Juggler • Lagoon • Lofty Peaks • Nocturne • Rhapsody Hongroise • Scherzando in G Major • Tango Carioca • Valse Burlesque • Valse Chromatique.

00111969 .... $12.99

LYNN FREEMAN OLSON – EARLY TO MID-INTERMEDIATE

13 Distinctive Piano Solos

Band Wagon • Brazilian Holiday • Cloud Paintings • Fanfare • The Flying Ship • Heroic Event • In 1492 • Italian Street Singer • Mexican Serenade • Pageant Dance • Rather Blue • Theme and Variations • Whirlwind.

00294720 ....$9.99

WILLIS MUSIC

EXCLUSIVELY DISTRIBUTED BY

HAL•LEONARD®

CLOSER LOOK View sample pages and hear audio excerpts online at **www.halleonard.com**

www.willispianomusic.com

 www.facebook.com/willispianomusic

Prices, content, and availability subject to change without notice.

CLASSICAL PIANO SOLOS

Original Keyboard Pieces from Baroque to the 20th Century

JOHN THOMPSON'S MODERN COURSE FOR THE PIANO
Compiled and edited by Philip Low, Sonya Schumann, and Charmaine Siagian

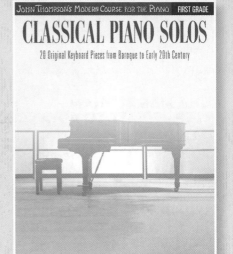

First Grade

22 pieces: *Bartók*: A Conversation • *Mélanie Bonis*: Miaou! Ronron! • *Burgmüller*: Arabesque • *Handel*: Passepied • *d'Indy*: Two-Finger Partita • *Köhler*: Andantino • *Müller*: Lyric Etude • *Ryba*: Little Invention • *Schytte*: Choral Etude; Springtime • *Türk*: I Feel So Sick and Faint, and more!

00119738 / $6.99

Second Grade

22 pieces: *Bartók*: The Dancing Pig Farmer • *Beethoven*: Ecossaise • *Bonis*: Madrigal • *Burgmüller*: Progress • *Gurlitt*: Etude in C • *Haydn*: Dance in G • *d'Indy*: Three-Finger Partita • *Kirnberger*: Lullaby in F • *Mozart*: Minuet in C • *Petzold*: Minuet in G • *Purcell*: Air in D Minor • *Rebikov:* Limping Witch Lurking • *Schumann*: Little Piece • *Schytte*: A Broken Heart, and more!

00119739 / $6.99

Third Grade

20 pieces: *CPE Bach*: Presto in C Minor • *Bach/Siloti*: Prelude in G • *Burgmüller*: Ballade • *Cécile Chaminade*: Pièce Romantique • *Dandrieu*: The Fifers • *Gurlitt*: Scherzo in D Minor • *Hook*: Rondo in F • *Krieger*: Fantasia in C • *Kullak*: Once Upon a Time • *MacDowell*: Alla Tarantella • *Mozart*: Rondino in D • *Rebikov*: Playing Soldiers • *Scarlatti*: Sonata in G • *Schubert*: Waltz in F Minor, and more!

00119740 / $7.99

Fourth Grade

18 pieces: *CPE Bach*: Scherzo in G • *Teresa Carreño*: Berceuse • *Chopin*: Prelude in E Minor • *Gade*: Little Girls' Dance • *Granados*: Valse Poetic No. 6 • *Grieg*: Arietta • *Handel*: Prelude in G • *Heller*: Sailor's Song • *Kuhlau*: Sonatina in C • *Kullak*: Ghost in the Fireplace • *Moszkowski*: Tarentelle • *Mozart*: Allegro in G Minor • *Rebikov*: Music Lesson • *Satie*: Gymnopedie No. 1 • *Scarlatti*: Sonata in G • *Telemann*: Fantasie in C, and more!

00119741 / $7.99

Fifth Grade

19 pieces: *Bach*: Prelude in C-sharp Major • *Beethoven:* Moonlight sonata • *Chopin*: Waltz in A-flat • *Cimarosa*: Sonata in E-flat • *Coleridge-Taylor*: They Will Not Lend Me a Child • *Debussy*: Doctor Gradus • *Grieg*: Troldtog • *Griffes*: Lake at Evening • *Lyadov*: Prelude in B Minor • *Mozart*: Fantasie in D Minor • *Rachmaninoff*: Prelude in C-sharp Minor • *Rameau*: Les niais de Sologne • *Schumann:* Farewell • *Scriabin*: Prelude in D, and more!

00119742 / $8.99

The brand-new *Classical Piano Solos* series offers carefully-leveled, original piano works from Baroque to the early 20th century, featuring the simplest classics in Grade 1 to concert-hall repertoire in Grade 5. The series aims to keep with the spirit of John Thompson's legendary *Modern Course* method by providing delightful lesson and recital material that will motivate and inspire. An assortment of pieces are featured, including familiar masterpieces by Bach, Beethoven, Mozart, Grieg, Schumann, and Bartók, as well as several lesser-known works by composers such as Melanie Bonis, Anatoly Lyadov, Enrique Granados, Vincent d'Indy, Theodor Kullak, and Samuel Coleridge-Taylor.

• The series was compiled to loosely correlate with the *Modern Course*, but can be used with any method or teaching situation.

• Grades 1-4 are presented in a logical and suggested order of study. Grade 5 is laid out chronologically.

• Features clean, easy-to-read engravings with clear but minimal editorial markings.

• View complete repertoire lists of each book along with sample music pages at **www.willispianomusic.com**.